GOING UNDER

BOOKS BY DONALD FINKEL

Going Under *and* Endurance 1978

A Mote in Heaven's Eye 1975

Adequate Earth 1972

The Garbage Wars 1970

Answer Back 1968

A Joyful Noise 1966

Simeon 1964

The Clothing's New Emperor 1958
(IN POETS OF TODAY VI)

A VENTURESOME THING

"It's a venturesome thing to explore," he said. "I guess we're all subject to it."

Stephen loved the cave
Floyd loved caving
Floyd was a caving fool

times he was gone two days running
trudging plunging leaping stumbling
loping clambering teetering creeping
slithering oozing grunting scraping
lay-back and chimney, straddle and belly-crawl
forcing leads and shifting breakdown

across bottomless pits
through corkscrews and chest-compressors
scrambling through the clammy shadow
a cave-rat, scuttling on all fours
panting, lantern in his teeth
came restless Floyd
lone mole of Barren County
sidling between thighs of limestone
groping her wet flanks
sleek with water, slick with clay

* * *

It was not till ten the next morning, twenty-four hours later, that young Jewell Estes crept within fifteen feet and called out. "Floyd?" It wasn't till late that night his brother Homer knelt by his head and wiped the mud from his eyes.

> *He was lying on his left side, turned somewhat on his back. Water was dripping steadily in on him from above, and there was no way for him to avoid it.*

Eight hours and two bushels of gravel later, Floyd's arms were still pinned to his sides. Homer crawled out for a few hours' breather. The water was dripping faster than ever.

* * *

DONALD FINKEL

Going Under

NEW YORK 1978 Atheneum

FOR RED AND PAT

Library of Congress Cataloging in Publication Data

Finkel, Donald.
Endurance: an Antarctic idyll.

I. Finkel, Donald. Going under. 1978. II. Title.
PS3556.I48E5 1978 811'.5'4 78-55020
ISBN 0-689-10902-4

Published simultaneously in Canada by McClelland and Stewart Ltd.
Manufactured by American Book–Stratford Press,
Saddle Brook, New Jersey
Designed by Harry Ford
First Edition

CONTENTS

What matters is that he wants to know what is there, and that he goes to see. R. A. WATSON

A LITTLE GROUNDWORK

All the caves mentioned by name in this book are now believed to be part of a vast interlocking underground network, running under two parallel ridges, namely Mammoth and Flint (and probably a third, Joppa Ridge), linked by narrow, muddy passages winding deep beneath the valleys between. On Sept. 9, 1972, when a connecting link was found between Mammoth and Unknown Caves, more than 144 miles of continuous passageway had been mapped. (Hölloch in Switzerland, the second longest cave in the world, boasted only 72.) As of the date of this writing, about 200 miles have been charted.

If you inquire as to the original discoverer of this vast subterranean wilderness, some will tell you a hunter named Houchins chased a bear into the historic entrance back in 1808. Others may point out marks of Indian torches on the walls, and mounds of charcoal from Indian fires. Evidence suggests the discovery occurred at least 3000 years before Houchins lifted his musket down from the mantelpiece. Throughout the cave there are countless signs of aboriginal mining, apparently for gypsum, and perhaps for mirabilite, a potent natural laxative.

During the War of 1812, the cave furnished the major source of saltpeter, mined almost exclusively by slaves, for the manufacture of gunpowder. Stephen Bishop, a slave, became one of the first, and the best-known, explorer-guides to Mammoth. When Frank Gorin, its nominal owner, sold the cave to Dr. John Croghan in 1837, he sold Stephen along with it. In 1842, the doctor attempted to set up a TB sanatorium inside the cave. All the patients died. Stephen continued to guide and to explore. According to one account, he dreamed of buying his freedom and emigrating to Liberia. Eventually his freedom was granted, but he died soon thereafter, and was buried near the cave.

We know of Floyd Collins chiefly on account of his untimely, unnecessary, and unaesthetic death, trapped in a passageway of Sand Cave, which he was exploring for purely mercenary reasons. While he lay dying underground, the great American journalistic circus flourished on the surface, complete with jugglers and balloons. I would prefer to remember Floyd for his discovery and extensive exploration of the magnificent Great Crystal Cave, which he struggled vainly for seven years to commercialize.

This poem, however, is not intended as a narrative dealing with the history of the cave area, but as a lyric exploration of the experience of "going under." The first section invokes Stephen Bishop for our guide, as we enter through Mammoth Cave. The second follows Floyd Collins through Great Crystal to Sand Cave, the scene of his last excursion.

* * *

I should like to express my gratitude to the members of the Cave Research Foundation, and in particular to Roger Brucker, Jack Freeman, Stanley Sides, Roger McClure and Armand Forster.

STEPHEN

down went the mustached Professor, the respectable merchant and the elegant Frenchman—each with his lamp swinging in its wire socket, and growing brighter as the gloom thickened—and I followed, with a cough which protested bitterly against the cold wind coming to meet us.

account of a visit to Mammoth Cave in 1852 by N. Parker Willis, in *Health Trip to the Tropics*

FOR WHAT

> *it was a common and human practice to employ laborers of enfeebled constitutions, who were soon restored to health and strength, though kept at constant labor; and more joyous, merry fellows were never seen.*

And that was 1812
for *laborers* read *slaves*
scooping peter-dirt into the ox-carts
singing, Hey he's long gone
Long John, with his long clothes on
while the oxen of darkness
jolted the earth to the leaching-vats, to feed
the famished cannon of New Orleans

whereas now on the road to the Job Corps camp
lounging on the soft green shoulder
disadvantaged, disabused, mostly black
in pairs and threes, they wait
for what?

which of them has broken into the ticket office
and stolen the candy, which of them
has ripped off two Coleman lanterns
for what?
and left them, empty
at the mouth of the cave?
where summer long she sighs
gently in the heat

her cool breath bathes your sweaty wrist

* * *

By 1813 the lifting of the embargo brought cheap saltpeter from the scented Indies. The curse of peace sent the gunpowder business down the drain in a sieve. Poor farms in the uplands, straddling the ridges, shagbark and poplar, sourwood, dogwood, not worth the plowing.

But they came from anywhere, suckers from Springfield, drummers from Memphis, beards from Cleveland and Cincinnati, blades and their Daisies, doctors of morphology, magisters of Latin, for Mammoth Cave. When Mr. Gorin bought her for five thousand in the summer of '38, he asked Shackelford and Miller, the reigning resident agents, sons of tenant guides before them, to take his young slave Stephen Bishop into the cave, to learn the routes and the spiel. A mannerly, mild, *au lait* Creole, smiling, articulate, seventeen, he was worth two field-hands and a mule.

* * *

GOING

Down the sinkhole
crashing through bracken
damp as a crotch
singing with mosquitoes
chiggers shimmering on the sandstone ledges
an oven-bird cries seven times, teaCHER teaCHER
teaCHER teaCHER teaCHER teaCHER teaCHER

quick now
under the chill spring, trickling
into the shadow, stumbling down the unstable
breakdown slope
dislodging stones

LIGHTING UP

Inside my lamp, in the double dark
water gathers like inward tears
dripping on the grey carbide
hissing an invisible blue
cloud of acetylene
that's tears against stone

cupping my hand on the bowl
I strike the flint
a needle of white flame
pops from the nipple
that's light against dark
that's stone against steel

I set the flame on my brow
and start down the slope
into the mines of possibility
trailing my lamp through Mummy Valley
something lovely that way goes
buoyed on an invisible river, knowing
there is hope and hope only
only a turning and returning
that's hope against hope

into the dark beyond dark
at the end of the passage
where all lights flicker and blink
out

* * *

They walked in silence, pale spheres mingling. Sixty feet above, the ceiling loomed, invisible. Sixty feet to either side, the walls invisibly rose. And sixty paces into the shadowy hall, they still could not make out the farther end. To their right hunched ruins of the leaching-vats, hulks of lumber, heaps of peter-dirt, broken picks. Deep into the mines of blood, Stephen drew the clean, clay-colored breath of breathing cave. His lamp guttered and flared.

Descending gradually, they found themselves on the floor of a gigantic limestone vault. Suddenly, Shackleford jabbed his neophyte. The young slave turned to see Miller behind them, but fifteen feet above, whirling his lamp on a ledge scooped from the wall like a natural pulpit, crying in a terrible voice: “Repent!” (“Pent, pent,” the walls replied.) Beside him, as if in answer, Shackleford snuffed his light. Up in the pulpit Miller’s winked and died. “Put it out!” a shadow rasped at his ear. Instantly, the rapt initiate bent to his lamp and blew, drawing the blackness around him like a blanket of sod, moist, palpable, voiceless, vast.

> *The grass must stop growing, and the stars hold their breath, to give you, above ground, any idea of that silence.*

* * *

HOW MUCH FURTHER

There are times when the Dead Sea, Styx, Lake Lethe,
Echo River and Roaring River combine into a swollen
stream fully two miles long, and how much further into
the depths nobody knows

Beyond Echo River
past Silliman's Avenue and Carneal Spring
past the vineyard of flinty grapes
in the lucid chapel on the hill
he knew, gazing into the farther room

(dark naked walls, like a charnel house
and, in the floor, carved from the living rock
an ample grave)

down in the river's roots, he knew
she was boundless, fathomless
great veins, thicker than cathedrals
and the deeper he knew, the freer he was

a bitter rain fell from the stalactites
muttering into the ears of stone
laid in primordial seas
the beds returned
stillness to stillness, grief to grief

in the room of columns
with one last tear
the ceiling married the floor

DATUM

Two and one-half meters north of B15 is a fecal specimen in situ on a ledge on the west side

Three hours down
there is a stone
which is not stone

in the cold light
of carbide it is
the color of dust

it shares with everything here
the dry metaphysical smell
of long-dead cave

curled serpent-wise on the ledge
head barely raised, it turns on me
its pointed eyeless stare

Old Ghost
I sing the morning
of your birth

a steaming snake
of acorns pokeweed
sumpweed panic grass

Grampa Fossil
Fusty Helix
teach me the way

*   *   *

By the time Mr. Stevenson turned up that October, Stephen had the routes by heart, eight miles of them under the ridge, and knew routes of his own. And the spiel. He could charm the teeth off dentists from Philadelphia, and their fine ladies. Now it was Stephen's turn to play schoolmaster. On the second morning, Stevenson, a ready proselyte

> *asked Stephen whether he knew of other passages where no man had gone before. Stevenson wanted to see some real cave. Yes, Stephen said, he knew where*

At the brink of the pit called Bottomless, Stevenson raised his arm to quell the wheeling shades of vertigo. Stephen plunged into the shadow, returning with two pole ladders, which he lowered, wedged securely, straddled, and shinnied across. Then it was Stevenson's turn. The long poles groaned, he caught the grace of fresh-cut cedar, keen as fear. All at once, he was over, reaching for Stephen's ready hand.

The passage slanted downward. They came to a muddy room where three leads crossed. Water called from afar like laughing children. Smiling, Stephen *père* stepped back as Steven-son led out, leaving vivid, unequivocal prints in the pristine clay. No one had been there since the birth of stone.

> *modern explorers have puzzled about the fact that just down the passage from the traditional cedar ladder crossing point, the gap narrows, so that one can easily climb across*

PRINTS

Ransack the apertures of night
for crumbs
a cricket
poised on the wall like a porcelain spider

the print of a naked human foot
a girl's
the shape of her passage
crisp as a leaf in the still cave air

leaning on a ledge, I leave
the print of my hand
clean in the fine dust and
plod onward in my powerful, easy
round-shouldered ice-age shamble

having signed my name
beside
FFS
1936
and
Wounded Bison
The Long Winter
and
Lost-a-Finger
who left his left hand on the wall
blowing earth-brown powder through a hollow bone

* * *

By the spring of '37, when Dr. Croghan came down from Louisville, Stephen had doubled the length of known passageway. The learned Doctor offered Gorin twice five thousand for the lot—land, cave and inn. Gorin couldn't resist.

The Doctor set out at once to graft an annex on the inn. The legislature voted him three fortuitous roads, from Cave City, Rowletts and Dripping Springs. There were trips into Mammoth almost every day for Stephen to lead. Striped trousers and a chocolate hat, a lantern, a basket of chicken and biscuits. Stephen came with the cave.

* * *

IT IS SAID

At the back of the cave
the wind god hunches with his mother
in their thatched hut
leaning their heads together
gross expressionless boulders
hacked by machetes

someone has planted
a branch of dead leaves by the door

at the back of the cave
spring day fall night the same
dank bearable season
neither rain nor thunder
drives their bison grazing peacefully
from the walls

wearies the antelope dancer
leaping in the yellow reedlight

*   *   *

> *have had Stephen busily employed drawing in pencil a map of the cave.*

Two bitter weeks that winter he sat at Dr. Croghan's table staring, not at the map, but the back of his head, walking it, crawling it, miles of cave unfolding in the nave of his skull, what did he call it? 'grand, gloomy, and peculiar.'

And every inch his pencil crept across the parchment, drawing her mysteries into the cruel white light of Louisville, cost him a year of his kingdom.

*   *   *

DEAD END

To consider the parts as passages
that go on
that pinch off
junctions, pits
belly-crawl, walking cave

where does it go?
on
how far is it?
where

under the cold white toes of
white-oak and hickory, nothing
but cave, cave, and
more cave

* * *

By Christmas morning of '42 there had sprung up, like a race of gargantuan fungi, seven cedar cabins and two stone huts, from Audubon Avenue to Wandering Willie's Spring, haunted by a tribe of ten consumptives, four paid companions, and a four-year-old boy. Dr. Croghan had established in the cave a hospital for consumptives, in the hope that she might be persuaded to render free men for a price what she had rendered slaves and oxen free.

* * *

THEIR HOPE

I am not sure that anyone has grown better but all concur in the opinion that they would be worse out, and hence contentment pervades our little community.

Rounding the Great Bend, Stephen
begins to hear it
the first faint clatter of musketry
steady, steadily louder till he is all but
struck down

in the halo of lamplight spilling
from the paneless window of the nearest hut
a woman kneels
by a stunted hawthorn, dying of darkness
in a bucket of sod

swathed in mole-grey wool
she blesses the desolate roots
from a bowl of water
in the second hut the coughing swells to a crescendo
blows of a tremendous sledge

Stephen raises his basket of partridge and greens
like a shield
or a sacrifice
beside him, Matt sets down his basket
leaps to the ledge, and winds his horn

Everybody saw and knew that they were tottering on the brink of the grave; and yet, such was their hope—a distinct and inseparable accompaniment of the disease—that they could not be persuaded to quit that purgatory.

trailing from the huts, a few creep round him
gazing with their great black irises while
fretfully against the ceiling writhes
a dragon of greasy smoke
Stephen can feel it sear her throat

how long before she coughs them up
demons, dragon, dining-hut and all?

* * *

> *his end approaching, the death-scene in that dark and silent abyss became so appalling, that they fled in terror—friends and servant—and left the dying man alone. Nothing could induce them to return*

Three died in the cave. All died within three years. And six years later, in 1849, the doctor, himself, died of the galloping cough, willing the cave to his descendants, in perpetuity. And willed Stephen his freedom, sweet as panther breath—but not yet. For another seven years, Stephen stayed in bondage, roaming his kingdom.

* * *

STAYING

and we will give you this also for the service which thou shalt serve with me seven other years

They will tell you he took a wife
a newspaper and a notion to emigrate
they will tell you he had a sockful of dollars
down there, jammed in a crack

they will tell you he stayed
more and more with the cave
not seven other years
but eight

she was drier, friendlier
than the rustling shucks
sun-cracks through cedar shakes
and nearer to Liberia

in the country of veins he ruled
over bats, blind fish
crickets and crystal
with a mild hand and a tallow candle

watching the shadow of his hand on the ceiling
reaching
pointing
breathing gently into the clay

NOCTURNE

On the thighs of silence I can make out
threads of frog-spawn
clusters of stone roe
rose-pale grapes

in the crevices, tendrils of gypsum
public mosses, spicules of mirabilite
fine as spider thread
furring the hollows

I run my finger down a cleft
between petals, tenderly
as if I were stroking
the lips of the dead

I have only to blow out my light
she will come to me
bare heels padding soft
as the beat of my blood

*   *   *

We were at the end of our journey—three P.M., and nine miles from daylight. The facile descensus Averni *had occupied six hours. Stephen had concluded his nine-mile lecture on geology, and sat waiting our pleasure. The Professor was examining a stalagmite. Our French friend smoked his cigar in silent contemplation; and the Bostonian, having managed to get behind the*

*   *   *

F L O Y D

Q.—Before you go any further, what would you term that place, a death trap?
A.—I call it Hell.

proceedings of the Military Court of Inquiry into the attempted rescue of Floyd Collins from Sand Cave, Feb. 12, 1925, Louisville *Courier-Journal*

CRYSTAL

At the foot of the sinkhole
I reach through the steel door
guiding the blind key into his cave

lock's stiff, the bolt complains, but they
stand back as we pass from the teeth of January
down April's throat
shutting the door behind us
and locking it tight

the trail of dead leaves gives out
and the chill
I feel her breath on my wind-bitten cheek
as we descend

in the room where the two rivers meet
where the canyons soar overhead, and the law
hangs upside-down like a bat
in a steel coffin bound with chains
lie the bones of restless Floyd

you can crack the lid
if I hold my light you can see
through the dusty glass
a wax mask, crazed but whole

from the sleeves of his black Sunday suit
two wax-pale gloves
fumble the shadow

in the vault of silence Floyd
lies on the floor like a
bad penny

* * *

8 AM, January 30th, 1925. Floyd followed the crest southwest, around Strawberry Valley, and came out on the road, scowling down the smooth black siphon that sucked the dollars into Mammoth. And a thin yet steady trickle into Great Onyx. But the few driblets that survived the spring-busting cowpath to Great Crystal Cave arrived at the ticket office vaporous, dazed.

* * *

FLOYD

> *Floyd had found a fine cave, and had developed one of the prettiest commercial tours in the region, but it became increasingly clear that the situation was almost hopeless. Tourists were out on the road to Mammoth Cave, but very few of them could be lured over to Flint Ridge.*

He was looking
not for the boundless but
a piece of the action
all he had to sell was holes

seven years in Crystal
(and one for the road)
clearing trails, waltzing boulders
moving time in the house of Persephone
making way
for what?

eight Januaries back, first time he felt her
warm breath on his knuckles
he wrestled a boulder from her mouth and
crouched awhile in the Kentucky dusk

> *went back to the house and casually asked his father whether he could have half the profits if he found a cave on the property with commercial poss*

in the land of his fathers
he found her
scouring the brush for a vagrant trap
stumbled into her open hand
and she was his

(no heelmarks in the sand

no charred reeds, torch-ties)
he knew every crease in her palm
he burrowed like a chigger into her wrist and
traced out her lifeline
by rights, she was his

eight bad years, mining a vein of
unenlightened self-interest
unreal estate

* * *

He turned and peered toward town. Cave City. Yes. They would have to pass here first. He would raise a whopping sign.

STOP HERE

FOR

THE CAVE!

He spun round, lurching into the underbrush. That road would be the death of Floyd.

* * *

ONE STORY

Sand Cave apparently is a common cavern, but in its vicinity are Mammoth and Great Onyx Caves, Colossal Cavern, Great Crystal Cave, Hidden River Cave, Horse Cave, Center's Cave, Dorsey Cave, Salts Cave, White's Cave, Dixon Cave, Proctor's Cave, Long Avenue Cave, Preston Cave, Highland Cave, Doyle's Cave of the Hundred Domes

She was everywhere beneath him
Flint Ridge, Mammoth Ridge
and she had to breathe
she had mouths everywhere for breathing
why not there? close to town
where the two ridges meet

One story is that Floyd worked his way through a very tight crawlway to the brink of a pit. He tied off a rope and went down. At the bottom he crept about 300 feet through a drain, and then turned to the left.

the walls sprang back
the ceiling reeled from
his lantern's reach

astounded
dumb as a boulder
he goggled her flowstone couch
her cut-glass and crystal
her glittering chandeliers
and beheld
through her glimmering nightgown
her creamy gypsum breasts
her spangled mound

she was there
where he knew she would be
the lantern muttered at his knee
a yellow seed in a great black fruit

he was coming back with the word
when the darkness
snapped shut on his foot

* * *

From her rotten jaw, a twenty-seven pound molar fell, nipping him neatly by the ankle. His lantern sprang from his hand, and sputtered out. Jammed like a cork in the crawlway, he couldn't reach the lantern or the rock with either hand. He yanked his trapped leg once, twice.

> *every movement brought loose material sliding into the crevice, solidly packing the space around his body. His hands were torn from clawing at the*

Twenty sweating minutes later, he paused. They would not miss him for eighteen, twenty hours, at least. How many times had he spent the night alone in Crystal, threading her dreamless maze? No one would think to look. He drew a deep breath, nestled his cheek in the breakdown, and settled to wait.

* * *

A MEAL IN THE MOUNTAIN

with peaceable Stephen and
restless Floyd
small, hunched
dining at the interface
at the skin of things

needn't look for us, Mother
we're here
one foot in the womb
wolfing indescribably
mangled Mounds bars
washed down with slash
our backs to the wall in the
gully of silence

three hundred feet from the nearest tree

* * *

And it was not till Monday morning that Skeets Miller, cub reporter for the Louisville *Courier-Journal,* scraped his painful way alongside Floyd with a small auto jack.

* * *

A WORD FROM SKEETS

Now fellow (this is what he calls me) you better go out and get warm. But come back. You're small and I believe you are going to get me out.

Small?
I mean

I was born in a sidewalk crack
in a beggar's pocket
he was small, like me

nose to toe, like fetal twins
I set the jack
and began to turn

It is significant to note that Collins' spirit seemed to snap when the jack failed to work. He began babbling incoherently and for the first time demanded that someone remain with him

in an aureole of sweat
hope and dripping stone
I set the jack again, again
for what?

I brought him a light so he
could see himself die
I warmed myself
at the furnace of his hunger
in the name of mercy and the fourth estate
I stuck my thumb in his agony
and pulled out a Pulitzer

bless the poor sod
let him lie

*   *   *

> *numerous campfires were burning atop the bluff. The snow which covered the ground was being melted by these fires and the water was running over the bluff into the cave. There were icicles hanging from the ledges.*

Hour on hour, tears of ground water gathered in a ceiling crack and fell, inexorably, on his right cheek, raced down his collar, leaching the crevices, sweetening Floyd.

How much was left for the crickets' dinner, lodged in the throat of darkness like a bone?

*   *   *

MY LIGHT

1:

You stroll off
into your own

turning to look back
your light bobs
high in the eaves of night
like a wandering star

I'm left with my light
nothing but what it lends me
dying

2:

My light needs tending
how right

setting my canteen on the ledge
in easy reach
and the plastic nursing-bottle
of fresh carbide
I lift the lamp from my brow
and blow it out

3:

For a long time
there is nothing
but the soles of my shoes

not even the faint
light of the stars
by which the sniper
finds his prey

yet my eyes continue
twitching in their boggy sockets
like tremulous eels

I hear the crickets
nibbling at my knapsack
I hear the earthworm
muttering among his geodes
lugging his tiny lantern of breath
sorcerer, soft as a lover's thumb

here sniff is king
and feel is queen

a fly circles, lost
buzing earnestly
comes to rest on my lips
thaws himself a while at my nostril
and leaves without saying

that's how we are

*   *   *

> *Things went from bad to worse as the National Guard commander took over.*

By the evening of the seventh day there had gathered an army, fifteen thousand strong. The fields around were drowning in Fords. On the bluff the cheerful bonfires blazed.

*   *   *

CARNIVAL

Jugglers and sleight-of-hand artists reaped a macabre harvest.

His brother Homer plowed through the rabble
muttering in his weeklong beard
—Where were you when he needed you?
picking his way among
pickpockets and preachers
guardsmen and concessionaires
peeping rubes and gaping samaritans
pimps, hucksters, suckers, seekers
moonshine and black balloons
marked SAND CAVE, to where
Lee their father straggled vaguely
more lost than Floyd

Then the ceiling collapsed in the passage, cutting Floyd off.

and where was Floyd when the roof fell in?
one foot under a stone already
ripe as a cheese in the seamless dark
flat on his back, singing
—Mother, I'm coming home

* * *

Lee Collins, his father, said tonight he had received a proposal from a Chicago booking office, offering Floyd a salary of $350 a week for a vaudeville tour.

* * *

HEARING THINGS

The last day on which anyone could say for sure that they heard a sound out of Floyd was Friday the 13th of February, on his 15th day in the hole.

I have heard that Floyd Collins seldom prayed. Perhaps so, but lying down there with him, clawing at the rocks around him, I heard him say prayers more beautiful than any I had heard before.

It seemed to me that I could hear him through the debris. Whether it was Floyd or not, I cannot say for sure. Under such conditions, alone in a cave, you may hear anything you listen for.

"Come on back to me," he shouted. "Come on back. I'm hungry."

When the purple mantle of light draped over the hills of old Barren County and the yellow incandescents gleamed far down in the yawning shaft, one could hear

Q.—A kind of loud, long breath?
A.—It was something like a groan; not a groan like you hear a man that gets hurt, in a hospital, you know.
Q.—A gasp?
A.—Yes, now you got it; now you got into my dictionary. If I brought my dictionary with me, I tell you a lot quicker.

OUR LIGHT

"Floyd's resting nicely," he said. "I've put an electric light by him."

Down Crystal, down
between boulders, a pint bottle
empty, a rusty nail
a racing stub, an opened can
matchbooks, gum wrappers and
everywhere, glinting in the breakdown
shattered glass
flash-bulbs, incandescent, soft-white
she eats our light and
spits out the shells

yet high on the walls, look
furring the scars of his
pick, where he hacked off
clusters of cave-grape
tendrils of calcium
to bless their mantels
with stolen fire

even now
she is healing

*   *   *

As his defenses collapse and his core temperature slides toward 85° F., his eyes glaze, and speech becomes slow, slurred and incoherent. The mind wanders drowsily, forgetfully

*   *   *

GOING

1:

Squatting for an hour at the bottom of his garden
rubbing shoulders with the boulders

lying under the ledge a year
grinning up at the lilies

petals of calcium, thorns of mirabilite
mushrooms and lily-pads

standing at the corner of Indian Avenue and Nameless Trail
watching the traffic

he could hear silence creaking on her pedestal
he could hear each grain

groan
as he shifted his weight to the balls of his feet

what light distinguishes, dark comprehends
in the democracy of dark

he felt her trickling her fingers down his groin
nuzzling with her hundred tongues

2:

He saw everywhere at once
racing down corridors
no one had trod
swimming through crevices
past the furthest
haunts of water

he was one with her everywhere
a worm meandering through a mountain
a mountain wandering through a worm
a stone that breathed
a sod that dreamed

but the dream was hers
stretching, turning
she smiled at herself in
the shuddering mirror of his mind

GONE

I saw what looked to be a boulder near his head, but it may have been his hand.

The dead have gone further down
seeking their level
ask ground water

they will tell you
when the shaft broke through
and Brenner made out
Floyd's slate-grey scowl in the rubble
he was two days gone

what was left of him could thread a needle
what his savior tugged at, retching
was broken meat

*   *   *

Oh how the news did travel
Oh how the news did go
It traveled thru the papers
And over the radio

*   *   *

BELOW ZERO

At the foot of the pitch
there's a hole by the wall
scraps of undressed lumber

(walk softly
Floyd's been here
scrabbling after whatever bone)

a log with a bark of nut-brown mold
mole-soft

come teach me patience, Great Crystal
my glittering muse
hard hat squats on my brow
like a limestone toad

When a dentist from Horse Cave bought Crystal off the old man, he borrowed Floyd, set him in the cave, in a proper box, welded steel with a plate glass top, so Floyd could see the tourists, gaping at the limestone sky.

> *The new tourist attraction—Floyd's corpse—was a sensation. The guides would lecture solemnly about the exploits of "the world's greatest cave explorer," and then the tourists would file by the body on display.*

*   *   *

LOOKING FOR THE DEAD

On March night in 1929, the resident manager and guides were startled to find that Crystal Cave had been broken into, the coffin opened, and Floyd's body stolen. Sounding the alarm, they fanned out around the entrance with bloodhounds to look for clues

They will tell you
next morning, at the base of the bluff
they found everything but the left leg
and popped it back in its box

slung between thieves
dizzy with moonshine, drunk with fear
how much of Floyd wafted down like a sack of bird-bones
from the top of the bluff

It was this way—you know, I have heard people say, "Well, I doubt his being in there at all."

(and where is the mummy of the princess
with her necklace of fawn-hooves
needles of bone and horn?)

they will tell you Floyd has
eaten his way through the bottom of three of the best
they will tell you
deep in the veins of Crystal
they have heard him calling
Wait for me

they will tell you the dead
will come again
climbing the roots of dandelion
riding the wild blue chariots of chicory
ask ground water

HOW RIGHT

I stroll up the slope
to the top of the canyon
rounding to the right
rising till my hard hat scrapes the ceiling

the passage narrows
but Floyd's made way for me
hacking off fingers and elbows of limestone
humping the breakdown on both sides
precariously

how right
where he stood erect, I stoop

> *The entry to Pech-Merle has such narrows, such abysses, such sliding cataracts of stalagmite, the chamber of Clotilde must be approached on hands and knees*

they begin to emerge on the ledges
temples of calcium
tiny columns and cornices
rococo scrolls and gypsum gargoyles
extravagant grottoes, gardens of crystal

Stephen, old potentate, I'm here!
each step, another kingdom
air's softer, and the floor
her red clay sucks my soles
with a ripe wet smack

> *In the Crystal Cave and in the Mammoth Onyx Cave, and in the Great Onyx Cave one is impressed everywhere with the evidence of* DESIGN. *Even the dullest minded cannot but wonder*

on the way down
I hold onto the hopes
Floyd nailed in her side
to keep from pitching into the pitch

how right

* * *

Washington, Feb. 16.—Years of effort to have the Federal Government develop Kentucky's Mammoth Cave as a National show place led the House today, following similar action by the Senate, to direct a survey of the Cave region, as well as

* * *

ASCENDING

from that tenantless yawn
I climb through the thick night layer
to all I own

whip-poor-will and honeysuckle
black jack, white-oak
the mazy moon

The speakers of the italicized passages are as follows:

PAGE 3 R. M. Bird
6 N. P. Willis
7 H. C. Hovey
8 P. J. Watson
9 (both) R. W. Brucker & R. A. Watson
12 Dr. John Croghan
14 (both) S. D. Sides & H. Meloy
15 Sides & Meloy
16 the authors of *Genesis*
17 Willis
23 Brucker & Watson
25 (1st) Louisville *Courier-Journal*
(2nd) Brucker & Watson
26 Homer Collins
27 Floyd Collins
28 Homer Collins
30 (1st) Skeets Miller
(2nd) H. W. Hartley
31 Homer Collins
33 Brucker & Watson
34 (1st) W. R. Halliday
(2nd) Brucker & Watson
(3rd) *Courier-Journal*
35 (1st) Brucker & Watson
(next two) Skeets Miller
(4th) Floyd Collins
(5th) Hartley
(6th) the Court of Inquiry
36 (1st) Skeets Miller
(2nd) Halliday
38 *Courier-Journal*
39 Rev. A. Jenkins & Mrs. I. Spain
40 Brucker & Watson
41 (1st) Brucker & Watson
(2nd) *Courier-Journal*

42 (1st) G. R. Levy
(2nd) H. F. Randolph
43 *Courier-Journal*

DONALD FINKEL was born in New York City and attended public schools there, notably the Bronx High School of Science. He studied sculpture at the Art Students League, and after earning a B.S. in philosophy and an M.A. in English at Columbia left the east for Illinois, Iowa, and finally St. Louis, Mo., where he is Poet in Residence at Washington University. He has lived for several years in Mexico, and travelled widely in the United States. He is married and has three children, three cats, and a Border Collie.

He is the author of *The Clothing's New Emperor* (1959), *Simeon* (1964), *A Joyful Noise* (1966), *Answer Back* (1968), *The Garbage Wars* (1970), *Adequate Earth* (1972) and *A Mote in Heaven's Eye* (1975). He has been the recipient of a Guggenheim Fellowship and a grant from the National Endowment for the Arts. In 1974 he received the Theodore Roethke Memorial Award for the book-length poem, *Adequate Earth.*

DONALD FINKEL was born in New York City and attended public schools there, notably the Bronx High School of Science. He studied sculpture at the Art Students League, and after earning a B.S. in philosophy and an M.A. in English at Columbia left the east for Illinois, Iowa, and finally St. Louis, Mo., where he is Poet in Residence at Washington University. He has lived for several years in Mexico, and travelled widely in the United States. He is married and has three children, three cats, and a Border Collie.

He is the author of *The Clothing's New Emperor* (1959), *Simeon* (1964), *A Joyful Noise* (1966), *Answer Back* (1968), *The Garbage Wars* (1970), *Adequate Earth* (1972) and *A Mote in Heaven's Eye* (1975). He has been the recipient of a Guggenheim Fellowship and a grant from the National Endowment for the Arts. In 1974 he received the Theodore Roethke Memorial Award for the book-length poem, *Adequate Earth.*

LASTING

1:

The distance to Husvik, according to the chart, was no more than seventeen geographical miles in a direct line, but we had very scanty knowledge of the conditions of the interior. No man had ever penetrated a mile from the coast of South Georgia at any point, and the whalers I knew regarded the country as inaccessible.

Silence, but for the sigh of their footsteps
three figures shuffle through the drifted snow
seeing neither northward the fretful sea
nor the rancorous crags blackening the south
down a tunnel of moonlight, sigh upon sigh

if twenty-eight men can drift to the end of their rope
in a year and a half
how many miles can three men creep
trailing behind them a thread of hope
each passing hour attenuates?

2:

—Are you game?

Down below us there was a precipitous slope the nature of which we could not gauge in the darkness, and the lower part of which was shrouded in impenetrable gloom.

three sit as one, astraddle
arms wrapped round the throat
of the one before

—Cast off!

three plunge as one
tobogganing into no-man's-land
wind thrusts his thumbs in the dreamer's ears

We seemed to shoot into space. For a moment my hair fairly stood on end. Then quite suddenly I felt a glow, and I knew that I was grinning!

3:

Three
in merciful stillness
in the lee of the rock

three glittering dimly, cowled in snow
limp as seaweed, numb as stone
cooling their heels on the threshold of death

one shudders
painfully straightens
gazing into the vortex

His idea was that we had trusted him, that we had placed ourselves in his hands, and that should anything happen to any of us, he was morally responsible. His attitude was almost patriarchal.

he could hammer a bent man straight
with a glance
pare a lop-sided oar with the edge of his smile

he cobbled from us
an ark of bones
and caulked it with blood

4:

during that long and racking march of thirty-six hours over the unnamed mountains and glaciers of South Georgia it seems to me that often we were four, not three.

Hunched with the weight of the dreamer
riding their shoulders
sharing their hooded vision
imponderous and palpable as moonlight
bowed with the weight of twenty-eight lives
four phantoms sleepwalk toward the gleaming uplands

5:

we listened intently. Then, clear across the mountains, in the still morning air, from eight miles away came the sound of the steam whistles of the whaling factories bidding the men turn-to.

no face; he has none, proper; nothing but that one broad firmament of a forehead, pleated with riddles; dumbly lowering with the doom of boats, and ships, and men.

Has the Sperm Whale ever written a book, spoken a speech?

Will he make a covenant with thee? wilt thou take him for a servant for ever?

Shall the companions make a banquet of him? shall they part him among the merchants?

into your hand are they delivered

6:

Presently our ears detected an unwelcome sound that might have been musical under other conditions. It was the splashing of a waterfall

From her drowse of stones the stream
plunges over the lip
into the boundless
the bottom falls away

first one
then another descends
through the chortling water
gasping and shining like minnows

then it is his turn:
hand over hand the dreamer
lets himself down
into the thundering

rope screams in his wounded hands his
toes strain for the ground as a
blow on the shoulder tears him free
plummeting into the grave of hope

As a process evolution defies (or contravenes) the second law of thermodynamics

lightning leaps from his heels and
sends him reeling into the light:
at his feet the water capers
on the rocks

sheathed in fluent
ice, the weeds
grin back at him
through the winking spray

7:

The blind endure their dark
the hills endure the stream
the battered child endures
loving the hand that wounds
the wife at her window endures
the snickering stars

the oak and the chestnut endure
enmity, tenderness
malice and charity
arrogance and pride
the worm, the dust, the years
the albatross and the dove

LAST

The rope could not be recovered. We had flung down the adze from the top of the fall and also the log book and the cooker wrapped in one of our blouses. That was all, except our wet clothes, that we brought out of the Antarctic, which we had entered a year and a half before with well-found ship, full equipment, and high hopes.

All but the bones, grandfather
dank as grave-mould
tough as elm

(as the great tree Yggdrasil
whose roots drink the streams of hell
in whose arms the stars are twittering)

a sail blinks round the cape into the bay
the boy is singing
the fisherman hauls the old man by his arm

dripping from the depths of sleep

The sources of the italicized passages are as follows:

PAGE 3 *Epic of Gilgamesh*
4 Minutes of Royal Geographical Society
5 Sir Ernest Shackleton (both)
6 Herman Melville, Shackleton
13 Harry McNeish, Shackleton
14 Melville
15 McNeish (both)
17 McNeish, S. T. Coleridge
18 Eugene Marais, Shackleton
20 Carl Sagan
23 Shackleton (both)
24 Shackleton, J. F. Hurley
25 Marais
26 Lionel Greenstreet, *Book of Genesis*
27 Louis J. Halle (both)
28 Halle
29 Shackleton, *Book of Job*
30 Frank Worsley, Shackleton
31 *Genesis,* Articles of the *Endurance,* Minutes of R.G.S.
35 McNeish
36 R. W. James, Greenstreet, McNeish
37 Shackleton, Dr. A. H. Macklin
38 McNeish
40 Halle
43 Worsley
45 *Gospel of Matthew, Gilgamesh, Book of Psalms*
46 Claude Levi-Strauss
47 Shackleton, McNeish
48 *Gilgamesh*
49 Shackleton
50 Worsley, Shackleton
51 Shackleton, Anonymous, Franz Boas
53 *Matthew*
57 Shackleton, Worsley
58 Worsley, Shackleton

59 Worsley, Melville (two), Job (two), *Genesis,* Shackleton
60 John Bleibtreu
62 Shackleton

I should like to express my gratitude to:

The Alexander Turnbull Library in Wellington, N.Z., for access to Harry McNeish's diary.

The Royal Geographical Society, for permission to reproduce the photograph of the *Endurance* on the cover, by J. F. Hurley, entitled "The Long, Long Night."

The Scott Polar Research Institute in Cambridge, England, for its kind assistance.

The National Endowment for the Arts for a grant covering part of the period during which this book was written.

Members of the Imperial Trans-Antarctic Expedition

Sir Ernest Shackleton	*leader*
Frank Wild	*second-in-command*
Frank Worsley	*captain*
Lionel Greenstreet	*first officer*
Hubert T. Hudson	*navigator*
Thomas Crean	*second officer*
Alfred Cheetham	*third officer*
Louis Rickinson	*first engineer*
A. J. Kerr	*second engineer*
Dr. Alexander H. Macklin	*surgeon*
Dr. James A. McIlroy	*surgeon*
James M. Wordie	*geologist*
Leonard D. A. Hussey	*meteorologist*

Reginald W. James	*physicist*
Robert S. Clark	*biologist*
James Francis (Frank) Hurley	*official photographer*
George E. Marston	*official artist*
Thomas H. Orde-Lees	*motor expert* (*later store-keeper*)
Harry McNeish	*carpenter*
Charles J. Green	*cook*
Walter How	*able seaman*
William Bakewell	*able seaman*
Timothy McCarthy	*able seaman*
Thomas McLeod	*able seaman*
John Vincent	*able seaman*
Ernest Holness	*fireman*
William Stevenson	*fireman*
Perce Blackboro	*stowaway* (*later steward*)